Minimalist Living

*How To Declutter Your Home, Let Go of
Unnecessary Things, Simplify Your Life,
and Find Happiness In What You Have*

Nick Anderson

Introduction 3
Chapter 1: What is minimalism anyway? ..10
Chapter 2: Why is Minimalism so Appealing?..27
Chapter 3: The 6 Principles of Minimalism 38
Chapter 4: Less is More............................41
Chapter 5: Let Go of Unnecessary Things .48
Chapter 6: Be Mindful of Your Priorities and Reset Them..55
Chapter 7: Redefine Happiness 66
Chapter 8: Choose to Edit Your Life.........76
Chapter 9: Clean Space is Vital.................87
Chapter 10: Best Practices 92
Conclusion..99

Introduction

To borrow a quote from the cult classic movie Fight Club, we buy stuff we don't need with money we don't have to impress people we don't even like. Does that sound familiar? It should. This statement pretty much describes modern life in the United States, Western Europe, Canada, Australia, New Zealand and many other places in the world.

The truth is no one country or culture has a monopoly on materialism and consumers. These two go hand in hand. Sadly, a lot is lost in translation. The truth is we have grown accustomed to assuming that the more stuff we have, the happier we are.

Americans are stuck on a frustrating mental escalator of wanting more, more and more. The truth is, when you look at any kind of advertising, it always comes back to one particular thesis. The thesis is actually simple.

If you want to be happy, get more stuff. If you want to feel fulfilled, get more stuff. If you want to feel appreciated, recognized and valued as a human being, you know what to do. That's right! Get more stuff.

It really all boils down to stuff and what it represents. Ad after ad, consumer message after consume message, we are trained to believe that if we want to gain the respect and admiration of people, if we want to feel fulfilled, if we want to feel happy, if we want to feel complete, we have to consume and consume and consume some more.

In fact, it's very easy to feel that the solution to whatever internal issues you are struggling with can be found in external solutions. If you want to be happy, buy stuff. If you want to feel fulfilled, gain the respect and admiration of people. If you want a sense of personal achievement, get even more with admirers.

The result is that we develop and unhealthy focus on more bright, shiny stuff and fame. The rise of social media did not help matters. It's not unusual for people to develop a really profound sense of narcissism because they're trying to compete with other people on their Facebook feeds or their Instagram accounts.

They're trying to present a picture to the world that they think other people expect of them. So when they see that their friends are traveling to all sorts of exotic locales all over the planet, they try to present the same impression. If they see that their friends have bought all sorts of expensive cars and gadgets, they try to keep up.

However, if they can't, it burns. They start thinking, "What's wrong with me? Why can't I have stuff? Why does it seem like everybody else is living a better life than me?" They feel left behind. They feel overlooked. They feel that there are so many things missing in their lives. At the end of the day, they feel defeated. They feel there's something wrong with them.

It is no surprise that given the rise of social media, America, as a whole, is feeling more lonely, depressed and anxious. In fact, in a February 2018 Gallup poll, more Americans report being depressed and suffering from anxiety than ever. This is not just a subjective thing, mind you.

This trend actually carries on the negative polling on mental health in 2017. In fact, if you look at pharmaceutical bestsellers in the past three decades, anti-depression and anti-anxiety medications are almost always near the top.

Those purchases never lie. There is a serious problem with issues of fulfillment and personal meaning in the United States. It's screaming out at you.

What really makes this so interesting is that it reveals the lie of materialism. All this unhappiness has happened even with an unprecedented rise in wealth in the United States. Indeed, in the year 2017, the number of millionaires living in the United States reached a whopping 10.8 million individuals.

Think about that for a second. Compare that to the population of the United States. That figure means that roughly one in thirty-one Americans is a millionaire. Despite this massive rush and explosion of wealth, gloom and loneliness and a lack of fulfillment flood the United States of America.

There seems to be a disconnect between the conventional wisdom that was taught to us by our parents that if you want to be happy, you have to achieve more, you have to earn more, you must have a lot more to show for yourself. That's how you become happy.

Well, there's a huge amount of millionaires, but there's also a very disturbing rise in suicides. You only need to look at the suicides of Anthony Bourdain and Kate Spade to see where this is headed.

The amount of money you have in the bank is not an antidote to a sense of being disconnected, lonely and unwanted.

A sense of meaning, fulfillment and purpose in this planet cannot be compressed into a capsule or a tablet. It cannot be sold over the counter or through prescription. It cannot be bought and sold online nor can it be shipped through Amazon.

It's something that has to come from within. Interestingly enough, more and more millennials, and I'm talking about people under the age thirty, are getting the memo.

They're beginning to realize that what they've been led to believe for all this time may not be all that hot. It may not be the right path. It may not lead to a happy ending.

It is not a surprise that a large chunk of Americans including many millennials are questioning the longstanding American happiness formula of more, more, more.

This book has no grand pretensions. I don't claim to know everything about minimalism. Instead, this book is a primer on how this idea and lifestyle can help you gain a greater sense of fulfillment and meaning in a chaotic and anonymous world. If anything, it aims to present you with another option.

You don't have to follow the path of more, more , more. You don't have to try to be something that you're not. You don't have to work yourself to the point you're almost burning out to chase after an illusion.

Instead of for trying to be something higher, bigger, better and trying to gain more and more stuff, the option of minimalism brings to the table is the idea that the less you have, the more you become.

Chapter 1: What is minimalism anyway?

Minimalism is quickly gaining in popularity especially among millennials. Minimalism has often been reduced to the tiny house movement, people living a nomadic lifestyle, people living out of their laptops. There are many threads to this. It's very easy to think that any one thread defines the whole movement.

Unfortunately, since it's still in its relative infancy, as far as social movement and lifestyles goes, there are many ways to define it and, ultimately, many of these will probably not withstand the test of time. It's in flux.

However, we do see broad outlines. We do see grand themes that unify most people's definitions of minimalism.

Before we dive into a working definition, here's a brief history. The word "minimalism" actually traces it's origin to the early twentieth century.

Usually, when people mention "minimalism", it's in the context of the arts and architecture. Usually, architects like Mies van der Rohe describe their work as minimalist; they're talking about large structures that are held up with the bare minimum of adornment.

If a wall is going to be busy or some other structural element is going to add too much volume to a structure, they try to leave it out. They focus more on the skeleton of the building which highlights the space that the building creates.

Interestingly enough, a lot of the architecture featured in the hit 1980s detective TV series Miami Vice was influenced by minimalism. It also had a lot of art deco houses, but there were a very significant percentage of minimalist houses and buildings featured in that show.

That's how most people first got into contact with minimalism. It was in the form of art or architecture.
The biggest proponent of minimalism was Ludwig Mies van der Rohe and the biggest designer who was really all about

minimalism was Buckminster Fuller. They not only participated in nailing down what minimalist art and architecture was and wasn't, but they also were quite instrumental in fleshing out the specific philosophy of minimalism.

At that stage, it could really be boiled down to one sentence "Owning less, consuming less".

The whole idea of minimalist architecture is to use as little materials as possible to take care of the basics. So, this means that when you live in a minimalist house, the building is not going to collapse on you. It's not like the architect saved on materials for the foundation and the main post for the house. No, it doesn't involve any of that.

Instead, there's a lot of glass, there's a lot of open space, but it's also a structurally sound unit. In essence, Mies van der Rohe was driving home the point that you don't need a lot for you to be taken care of.

You can get that big space. You can get that light. You can get that inspirational atmosphere. You can get a meaningful space around you.

However, it doesn't have to involve a lot of stuff. You don't have to beat yourself up in terms of packing as much material into the same space as possible.

This leads to the revolution that other items can be minimalist as well. Take a phone, for example. It doesn't have to eat up so much steel, plastic and rubber. It can be very streamlined. It can be just like a thin metal rod with a receiver and a speaker.

This kind of thinking really blew a lot of people away in the early twentieth century because you have to understand this was near the tail end of the industrial revolution. When the industrial revolution blew up in England, there was a massive explosion of wealth.

People were under the impression that the more stuff you have, the wealthier and more important you are. Everybody was focused on getting. Everybody was focused on taking and taking and taking.

So, what happened as far as designed went? Well, when you look at the stuff designed then, everything was bulky. Everything was huge.

Take the case of the telephone. I mean, if you've seen a telephone from the 1800s, it's huge. It has a thick speaker, it has a thick transmitter. The same applied across the board.

When minimalism entered the scene, everything got stripped down. There was a rush to look at the very basic functions of the item being designed and zero in on that with the least amount of materials.

It turned out by zeroing in on the basics, you actually tease out a lot of elegance and sophistication. When you look at a Mies van der Rohe building or, to a lesser degree other architects at that time, you get a sense of sophistication.

It's not trying to be something that's not. It's not trying too hard. But its simplicity radiates elegance.

In other words, Mies van der Rohe reinterpreted what it means to be classic. You don't have enter a room and blow everybody away by how rich you are. You don't have to put on a show.

People can just see in the simple economy of how you move and how you carry yourself that you are a person of importance. That's the kind of effect minimalist architecture had.

Interestingly enough, other architects who are not normally associated with minimalism like Frank Lloyd right reflect some of that in their work.

So, minimalism, at this point, was primarily an artistic and architectural movement, but it was part of a questioning attitude regarding the whole idea of more, more, more.

Minimalism incorporates Zen Buddhist and stoic beliefs

Let's get one thing clear. When minimalism started, it was primarily a design philosophy, but people saw the value in its questioning of the dominant consumer philosophy of Western Europe and the United States.

It is no surprise that it quickly drew the attention of people who had backgrounds in Buddhism and Roman stoicism.

Stoicism has always been around. In fact, a good argument could be made that it was the official philosophical "religion" of the Roman era. You have to remember that when it comes to actually religion, during the Roman times, people were pagan so there were different gods. A lot of them came from the East or from Egypt. So, when it comes to actual religious beliefs, creeds and doctrines, there are dozens to choose from.

However, when it comes to the actual attitude or ethos that religion often brings to the table, stoicism was it. You only need to look at the emperor Marcus Aurelius to see how stoicism guided his life and inspired people around the emperor.
This was how you were supposed to live, and the interesting thing about stoicism is that it actually acted at some sort of antidote to the excesses of pagan times. Make no

mistake if you were a freeman during Roman or Greek times, you can pretty much to do whatever you want. You can kill a slave with impunity. You can have sex with your female slaves. If your wife has a kid and you don't like the kid, you can have the kid killed.

That's how much power there was at that time. It's as if the Judeo-Christian rules that we have grown so accustomed to seemed so foreign back then. There was so much inequality, so much power concentrated in the freeman that it was really crazy because there were no really boundaries. You can do whatever you want, and this took particularly barbaric form when it comes to conquests.

When the Roman armies, for example, conquered a territory and you were on the losing side, better run for the hills because you don't want to see what they're going to do to you if they get their hands on you. Crucifixions were common, but that just the tip of the iceberg.

In light of all this free-wheeling, chaotic, do-it-if-it-feels-good-do-your-own-thing environment, stoicism flourished.

The interesting thing about stoicism is that it was popular precisely because it's what you're supposed to do. Stoicism is all about freedom from the attachment to comfort. This really is quite an interesting philosophy because it flies lives in the face of the tremendous and unprecedented comfort and convenience the Roman Empire made possible.

It was a very rich empire with all sorts of products and social arrangements. It was very elitist. In fact, you know you're a rich person and you occupy the top of the food chain based on how much power and possession you have.

Stoicism turned its back on this. Life is not supposed to revolve around comfort. It understood life for what it truly is. Life can be chaotic. There's a lot of pain in life. Life is unfair.
Accordingly, simplicity and clarity and doing much with very little were very high on the stoic value hierarchy.

Interesting enough, this coincided hand and glove with the other train of thought in forming minimalism, which is Zen Buddhism. In fact, a lot of designers who call themselves minimalists were very much aware of Zen Buddhist design.

Zen Buddhism is very big on simplifying concepts to the bare minimum.

If you need a good example of Zen design philosophy, look at the Japanese flag. It's not very busy. It just has a white field and a red circle.

That is Zen. It's supposed to represent the sun, but it's very singular, it's hard to miss and it makes its point. In other words, it's able to do a lot with very little. Sounds very stoic.

This is why Zen Buddhism and stoic beliefs really fused within minimalism because now, people have a philosophy of getting rid of as much material as possible initially with design.

As minimalism lets you get rid of things, materialism pushes you to gather things. As more and more designers adopted a minimalist attitude, they started looking at their design choices and asked themselves, "Am I just going through the process? Am I putting this element in because that's what's expected of me? What if I take out that wall? What if I move that post?"

This brought home the point that the value of something, first in design and later in people's lives, is not so much whether you're supposed to have it there at that spot, but more of why you should put it there in the first place.

What is the ultimate purpose? What is the core of that design element? Is it load-bearing? Does it have a very compelling function? If not, you can take it out. It's not a deal-killer.

This reflects this awesome mixture of stoicism and Zen Buddhism because the essence of Zen Buddhism is still Buddhist doctrine, which is freedom from attachment. When you are able to move things around, you're not as attached to them because you don't have to do them out of obligation. There's nobody to impress. There's no checklist to go through because it's not absolutely essential.

Similarly, stoicism teaches that it's okay to free yourself from attachment to comfort. So, even if that wall has a function of keeping you comfortable, you can let go.

Ultimately, with stoicism in the picture, the comfort that you're letting go is the comfort provided by conventional wisdom, tradition and other people's expectations.

Put all together and simplified into its most pure thesis, minimalism can be an antidote to modern consumer trends like the following:

Fusing identity with material possessions

Did you know that youth movement in the United States and elsewhere determine who's in and who's out of the group based on what you own? People who are into the punk movement can easily tell whether you're a punk or not based on the clothing you're wearing.

Since you own your clothes, your possessions define you. It's as if these material possessions act as some sort of uniform. Sooner or later, they become fused with your identity. You can tell who's a preppy. You can tell who is an emo, you can tell who's a goth, you can tell who's into rockabilly, so on and so forth.

This does not just involve youth movements or musical preferences, mind you. This applies across the board. Your identity flows from what you own. We've crossed the threshold where we've gone from possessing things to things possessing us.

Deriving happiness and fulfillment from things we own

Not only can things define our identity, they are also often read as sources of fulfillment and happiness.

According to a recent study on the psychology of possessions, researchers discovered that when people buy stuff, they actually get a sense of fulfillment. On that narrow point, money can buy happiness. When you by a new pair of Air Jordans, you feel happy.

But here's the complication. When compared to experiences, buying things to make you feel happy doesn't last. In fact, the more stuff you buy, the less fulfilled you become. You still feel happy, mind you.

When you buy new stuff, there's something to celebrate. You feel good. You bought a new car, new shoes, new furniture, but that thrill goes away fairly quickly.

Interestingly enough, when you spend your money on a vacation, the happy memories of that vacation persist a longer time. The conclusion of the study was pretty straight forward. If you're going to be buying happiness, try to buy experiences.

Still, this study highlights the fact that people can derive happiness and fulfillment from the things they own. This is really just a restatement of what many people already believe.

However, here's the problem. It's temporary. That is the startling revelation of that study.

This means that if you are going to get your social happiness and fulfillment solely from stuff you can buy, you are trapped in a hamster wheel. You're going to have to continue to buy, buy, buy before the rush wears off. So, you're stuck like you're addicted to this drug that you have to keep taking; otherwise, the rush will disappear and you're forced to wake up.

People don't get that part. Instead, they celebrate the stuff they own. They stop there, but they don't see the whole picture. They don't understand that you have to keep buying, and once that buying process stops, you get depressed. You feel unworthy. You feel defective. You feel there's something missing in your life.

Self-definition must use external measures

The third consumer trend that minimalism counteracts is the idea that happiness can only come from outside of you. Whether it's buying stuff or measuring happiness or factors that improve happiness, all of it has to come from outside you.

Taken to its logical conclusion, this leaves powerless. They feel that they are at the mercy of the stimuli that's out there. If everything doesn't line up properly, they're not going to be happy.

This leads to a profound sense of lack of control. It is no surprise that suicide rates are going up. It is no surprise that the sense of depression, the sense of loneliness and lack of meaning has reached such a high level in the United States because, ultimately, we can't keep pulling in stuff from the outside world. Eventually, we have to confront this deep pool of unhappiness and discontent from within.

However, unfortunately, that's the kind of mirage or illusion set up when we believe that our happiness must come from outside. This really prevents us from taking ownership and responsibility over our ability to be happy. It obscures the fact that it is a choice.

Thankfully, minimalism is growing and it continues to be redefined in such a way that it stands to reach a wider of audience of people. And not a minute too soon.

Chapter 2: Why is Minimalism so Appealing?

Minimalism is quietly growing among a significant section of America and Western Europe's population. In fact, this is an international trend.

It's just more pronounced in the so-called developed world. It is most popular among millennials. Minimalism's appeal is pretty much fed by many different trends.

Several years ago, there was an occupy Wall Street movement in the United States. The idea was that there is a predatory ruling class that is pretty much eating up all the resources of the world.

This is a very distinct political view, not exactly new, but there's definitely a lot of energy in that movement. It found its voice with the candidacy for the Democratic Party's presidential primary of Senator Bernie Sanders from Vermont.

The idea is that there is something fundamentally wrong, or even sick, with how Americans taught about wealth, where wealth comes from, and how societal resources should be handled.

Now, you don't have to share that political philosophy to sympathize with the underlying assumption that there should be an alternative to the consumer's model of more, more, more.

While the Bernie Sanders campaign has come and gone, there is the awareness that it raised in many people, regardless of political Stripe, remains to this day. There is a questioning attitude regarding how we should define ourselves, what we should strive for, and what ultimately, is the meaning of life. It all boils down to priorities.

One thread that came out of that question is minimalism, as applied to lifestyle and life choices. Minimalism allows you to get rid of things that have limited value, no use, or are distractions to the things that you should be paying attention to.

It frees you up so you can focus on things that are relevant and truly help you become a better use, not only to yourself, but to other people. The driving force behind this idea is the desire for freedom.

It seems that for many people, they no longer own their possessions. Instead, their possessions or, more specifically their need for possessions, have possessed them. When you declutter or let go, you gain, not only material or physical place, but also personal, mental, and emotional space.

There are less things to worry about. There are less things to focus on, in terms of maintenance, insurance, credit card payments, and other long-term commitments.

You have to understand that a large of bulk of the consumerism in the United States is not funded by ready cash. People don't have that kind of money. Instead, they leverage their future to pay for things now.

That's right. They use their credit card. It is no surprise that as of this writing, America's total credit card debt is way over one trillion dollars. Let that sink in. One trillion dollars.

That's roughly three thousand dollars per head, if you were to distribute it among the entire population of the United States. I'm also including in that figure kids, infants, toddlers, and senior citizens. That's a lot of money. That's a lot of debt. That's a lot of worrying.

It's no surprise that minimalism is fast growing. It's expressing itself in many different forms.
People want more control over their lives. Last time I checked, you don't really have that sense of control when at the end of every month, you get a fat credit card bill.

Guess what? If you choose to only pay the minimum. That balance only gets bigger and bigger. Minimalism also frees people from an unhealthy obsession with materialism.

One of the reasons we suffer from mental and emotional clutter is the compulsion to get more and more stuff. It's not unusual for people to develop some sort of hoarding compulsion.

You go to sale after sale. You buy all sorts of stuff and put it in your closet. Your closets fill up, so you buy even more closet space.

Lost in this equation is the reality that, for the most part, you don't even use a large percentage of the stuff you buy. Buying stuff on sale is what motivates you. Using that stuff is not really on the radar.

A lot of people tend to use a certain range of clothing, accessories, and gadgets. What happens to the rest? Well, they sit in their closet until spring cleaning comes around, maybe after five years. That stuff gets sold at a steep discount at a garage sale.

If you suffer from this, what you're really buying is not an item. It's not another coat that you're going to use. It's not another gadget that you're going to use. It's something else.

You're buying the rush that you get from getting something at a big discount. That's what you're buying. You're buying a feeling.

As I mentioned earlier, according to a research study, led by Professor Andrew Jebb from Purdue University that published in Nature Human Behavior, people buy stuff to be happy and it does work. That's right.

When you buy things on sale, you get that nice rush. It's real. It's not just in your head. However, the problem is it doesn't last. So, you buy more and more and more. You get desensitized.

Ironically, what you're really buying is the experience. According to Professor Jebb's research, you'd be better off buying experiences outright.

Take a vacation. Go to school. Go to training seminars. Go hiking or camping. Even then, the sense of fulfillment and happiness erode over time.

The bottom line is you can't buy this. You can't buy permanent fulfillment. It's just not going to happen. Unfortunately, human beings being human, focus on a straight path or the path of least resistance for their problems.

It takes time to plan a trip. It's much easier to just buy stuff so we're stuck in that acquisition mindset.

True happiness

Another benefit minimalism brings to the table is that it takes us closer to true happiness. Too many people think that happiness is something that comes outside of you.

They think that it's something that has to happen to you and that it comes from the outside and works its way in. It's actually the other way around.

When you shift to minimalist lifestyle, you focus on the things that you experience within. You focus on how you perceive things.

You focus on the special moment or the feeling of the moment when you're helping other people or when other people are helping you, when you're resolving conflicts, and when you're forgiving or being forgiven. These don't cost money.

Often times, these don't have a material element to them. Instead, it's about being in the moment. It's about interacting with people on a sincere, authentic, and real level.

I wish I could tell you that it's always possible. I wish I could tell you that this is all smooth and easy, but it isn't.

Often times, for you to reach that stage of peace, harmony, and mutual understanding, you have to overcome conflict, disagreement, and emotionally upsetting exchanges with people. Regardless, it's internal.

It doesn't come from outside. It's not some sort of product that you pick out at a store. It doesn't work that way. Ultimately, happiness is a choice. It can come from a memory.

Resource efficiency

Another benefit people get from minimalism is that they're able to save resources. When you become less materialistic, your money is shifted somewhere else.

Maybe you save and invest it. Maybe you buy experiences or invest in your personal knowledge and development.

Whatever the case may be, you spend less on stuff. This alone, should make people sit up and pay attention. As I mentioned above, Americans have an aggregate credit card balance of over one trillion dollars.

Can you imagine the interest on that? The annual percentage rate interest for the average credit card is over 12%. We're talking about one trillion dollars here with an average 12% interest rate. You do the math. It's scary.

When you become less materialistic because of minimalism, you don't join that sorry statistic. You can even grow your money.

Saving time

What if I told you that your most important asset is not in the form of the green pieces of paper in your wallet? What if I told you that the most important financial building block that you can work with is not expressed in the figures that you see when you log in for online banking?

Your most important asset is your time. Whatever you invest your time in grows. If you invest it in learning, you eventually become an expert.

If you invest it in relationships, your friendships deepen and your relationships grow. If you invest time in your health, you become leaner, faster, and you achieve a greater sense of well-being.

However, when you spend time on consuming stuff, the return on effort that you get is very, very bad. Why?

Sure, there's a reward. When you look for stuff online, you get rewarded by the thrill from buying something new. However, as I mentioned earlier, that thrill is temporary. Too temporary.

You have to find something else. When you stop running fruitlessly on the rat race treadmill of life, you can devote to things that truly matter— self-development, relationships, caring for others, and caring for your community.

These actually help give you more meaning. Interestingly enough, it can actually lead to you making even more money.

Funny how that works right? Please note all the advantages of minimalism I've listed above. This is just a short list.

The bottom line is if it resonates with you on a deep and personal level, then it's definitely an option you should take. In the next chapter, I'm going to get in the nitty-gritty of the six principles of minimalism.

Chapter 3: The 6 Principles of Minimalism

Minimalism enables you to let go of unhealthy obsessions and priorities. It enables you to live life with more control and freedom.

To get to that point, minimalism uses 6 principles. You don't have to follow all of these, but to live a minimalist lifestyle and possess a mindset that enables you to achieve many, if not all, of minimalism's benefits, it would be a good idea to subscribe to and live out these principles.

These are not just philosophical statements, mind you. They all have practical implementations.

Principle #1: Less is More

Principle #2: Let Go of Unnecessary Things

Principle #3: Be Mindful of Your Priorities and Reset Them

Principle #4: Choose to Be Happy

Principle #5: Edit Your Life

Principle #6: Space is Vital

In the following chapters, I am going to expand on what these principles mean and give you some examples of how you can implement them in your life.

Again, you don't have to adopt all 6 all at once. You may want to start with one. You may want to play around with it and see how it applies to your particular set of circumstances. Once you get the hang of it, you can then go down the list and apply it to your life.

Now, please understand that there is no one-size-fits-all, magic bullet type of solution here. This is not like some sort of product that is standardized and applies to all people the same way at all times. It doesn't work that way.

These are just principles. Meaning, at the end of the day, you are in control. You have to fit these principles based on how your life actually is.

You might have to make some adjustments, or you may have to apply it in certain situations differently. Whatever the case may be, you need to start on these if you want to enjoy the many benefits minimalism brings to the table.

Chapter 4: Less is More

This principle flows directly from Zen Buddhism. Zen Buddhists believe in the principle that less actually produces more results. When you have less, you can actually enjoy more things.

On a practical level, this can be applied to the concept of clutter. Clutter has two dimensions: there is physical clutter, and mental or spiritual clutter.

Physical clutter is very easy to see. It's stuff that you have all over the place.

If you have an office, it's probably the stacks of paper that you have around you. If you look at your living room or your bedroom, it's probably the clothes or all the other stuff that are strewn all around you.

Even if you are a very neat person and you make sure that everything is folded and stored away, you can still be in a cluttered environment. Why? There's so much stuff in storage.

You know that you have that stuff. They might not be physical clutter that people can see, but there sure is mental clutter because you worry about your stuff.

You worry about maintaining them, you worry about paying for them, you worry about losing them. You worry, and worry, and worry.

Clutter never stops being clutter the moment you don't see it. You may have put it away, you may have put it in storage, but that fact alone doesn't make the clutter go away.

Remember, clutter has two dimensions. It can be physical and emotional or spiritual. These two go hand in hand. Still, you will be in a better position if you got rid of physical clutter.

For example, if you have lots of stuff around you and there's not much space to work with, it can lead to a tremendous amount of emotional stress and pressure. It's not obvious, it's not like you're doing it intentionally, but if you're not careful and you let stuff pile up around you, you're not doing yourself any favors.

You're already dealing with all sorts of pressures, deadlines, timelines and whatnot. When you see all this clutter, your sense of urgency gets distorted. Your ability to focus gets thwarted or gets misdirected.

Whatever the case may be, it plays a trick on you. Instead of being able to look at your to-do list and handle one thing at a time, it's very easy for your focus, and by extension your willpower, to get diluted or diffused because you have so much stuff around you.

The great thing about physical clutter is that it's fairly easy to deal with. You just need to clear it up.

If you have lots of stuff on your bookshelf and most of them are not books, you know what to do. Whip out a box, take those items off your bookshelf, and decide what you're going to do with the items in the box. If you have stuff on the floor, pick them up.

Physical clutter, by and large, is very easy to handle. There's really not much mystery behind them. Still, the positive effects of clearing up physical evidence is quite convincing.

In a Princeton study conducted in 2011, test participants were put in a cluttered room and then they were asked to do certain tasks. When the participants were asked to do stuff that's irrelevant to the main task that the subjects were supposed to do, the images of the subjects' visual cortex showed a tremendous amount of activity. This correlated to their reduced ability to focus and complete the task that was assigned to them.

The conclusion was clear: clutter makes it so much harder for you to focus so you can get stuff done. Clearing up that clutter enables you to focus better.

Similarly, in a National Institute of Health report in 2010, cleaning up clutter or the inability to deal with clutter, can have an impact on a person's mental state. They can be depressed.

In fact, in the study first published in the Personality and Social Psychology Bulletin, women who describe themselves as living in cluttered surroundings or living around unfinished projects self reported higher levels of fatigue and depression compared to women who described their surroundings as restorative and restful.

Finally, in an Indiana University study performed by researcher Nicole R. Keith, individuals living in clean houses tended to be healthier than those living in cluttered surroundings.

Make no mistake, clutter can stress you out. It takes up a tremendous amount of focus, it makes it so much harder for you to take care of what you need to do, and it leads to emotional and spiritual clutter. One manifestation of this, of course, is depression.

As the study reported in the National Institute of Health and first published in the science journal Personality and Social Psychology bulletin, your mental state can suffer tremendously because of clutter.

Again, clutter operates in two dimensions. Don't think that physical clutter doesn't affect you. It does affect you internally.

This can also work the other way. If you feel mentally cluttered and you're unable to do much of anything because you feel that you're just trying to keep on top of so many duties, obligations and responsibilities, don't be surprised if stuff starts piling up around you.

If you feel that you just don't have the time to keep your surroundings clear, this in turn stresses you out even more because you see all this stuff around you. It's a vicious cycle.

The key is to understand that less is more. You don't have to have all that stuff. The cleaner your surroundings, the more restful you would feel. It all boils down to making a decision to clear stuff out.

The worst part about all of this is that people tend to let clutter pile up around them because they feel that they can't let go. They kind of treat their possessions as sources of comfort. They look at them as symbols of a sense of control.

And that's what's ironic about it because it doesn't lead to control. You feel that you don't have the time to clean up everything. You don't feel in control when you have that mindset.

And then it stresses you out. But you can't let go. You can't clear stuff out. You don't even know where to begin.

But if you want to adopt a minimalist lifestyle, you have to decide that less is more. Start with the clutter you can see, and you'd be surprised how it would quickly lead to you becoming free of the clutter you cannot see.

Chapter 5: Let Go of Unnecessary Things

A lot of Americans have a tough time letting go. They really do. They have a tough time getting rid of stuff, and it's very easy to see why. It's not like the stuff is free.

You worked hard for that stuff. You worked hard for your money. You traded in time, focus and energy to get the money to buy stuff, now you're going to have to let them go? This is where the resistance comes in.

Believe it or not, even though you don't live in a cluttered space, you can can still have a problem with your possessions because you're simply hanging on to too much stuff. There is such a thing as hanging on to too many things.

Even if there is no clutter, even if somebody comes to your house and it's obvious to them that you're not some sort of hoarder, you may still need to let go. Why? Well, it leads to mental cramping.

Sure, that car that you bought for $100,000 may not be in your living room or your bedroom, but you can bet that if you're making payments on that car to the tune of thousands of dollars every single month, it's going to mentally take up some real estate. Do you see where I'm coming from?

And the more you do this, the more unhappy you become. You become stressed, anxious, and worst of all, you feel like you're stuck. You feel like you're tied to that thing that you constantly worry about.

When you're not worrying about it getting stolen, damaged or misplaced, you're worried about paying for it. If you're not worried about where the money is going to come from, you're worried about maintaining it.

There's only one thing constant in that line of thought: you worry, worry, and worry some more.

Let go of unnecessary things. We're not talking about clutter anymore. We're talking about stuff that is simply weighing you down because you think so much about the consequences of possessing it that it tires you out.

Usually, this is the house. This should not be a surprise because residential property in the United States is the main form of most Americans' wealth.

In a recent report, 10.1% of Americans as of the year 2017 are millionaires. What that report doesn't say is that it's a net worth assessment. Meaning, people don't make a million dollars a year. Instead, their net worth is over $1 million.

In practical terms, this means that their real estate holdings are worth that much.

Understand how this works. Understand what form your wealth takes.

This means that, in practical terms, people tend to worry about their home. They're worried about property taxes, proper maintenance, water boilers breaking, you name it.

And it's very hard to let go because you feel like you're just being a responsible adult.

You're just taking care of issues as they arise, but this leads to a tremendous amount of stress.

You're giving up a lot the more you hang on to things. And you're not physically hanging on. This is happening mentally.

Now, please don't misunderstand me. I'm not saying that you should move out of your house and sell it. What I am saying is that you should create a list of the things that you own that take up a lot of your mental processing power. You'd be surprised at the things that are on that list.

Once you have that list, maybe it would be time for you to look at your priorities and consider letting some of that go. It really all boils down to the concept of "necessity."

I wish I could tell you that there is some sort of bright line answer, but there isn't. What you consider a necessity may be a luxury to me, and vice versa. Only you can answer this question. Only you can supply the definition.

Regardless, you need to get rid of unnecessary things because if you do, you get a greater sense of freedom. You're no longer doing mental heavy lifting when you let go of stuff that used to take up a lot of your thoughts. This frees you up to live for the moment, enjoy the moment, and, believe it or not, become happier.

In a UCLA research study reported in 2013 by the New York Times, 32 Los Angeles families were studied. The mothers in those families had their stress hormone levels measured.

This is a very important study because this is not just self reporting your emotional state. The researchers actually took your blood samples to see objective indications of real stress.

It turned out that when these women were dealing with anything related to their belongings, the amount of stress hormones in their blood spiked up.

The researchers concluded that when you have physical clutter, your senses get overloaded and this stresses you out and reduces your ability to creatively think. Letting go of unnecessary things can definitely help.

Of course you can't go overboard. You can't just renounce everything overnight and become some sort of instant hermit. That's too much of a break.

But you may want to wean yourself off. You might want to start off with that list. Right off the top of your head, list down all the stuff that you think about every single day. Be perfectly honest.

Again, there's no right or wrong answer. The only person that will know whether the answers are right or wrong is you.

Be completely honest with yourself. And then once you have done that, give yourself some time to look at the list when you're not stressed. Look at the list when you're in a relaxed environment.

Things should fall into place. The picture should become very clear. It should be obvious that you are spending a tremendous amount of your mental processing energy on things that are not necessary.

So at that point, you might want to start prioritizing. There are certain non-negotiable things on that list to be sure. However, there's also stuff that is obviously more bother than they are worth. Know the difference.

Chapter 6: Be Mindful of Your Priorities and Reset Them

Let's get one thing clear, you cannot prioritize "happiness." That's too tall of an order. It really is.

Why? Well, let's be honest. The way we normally define happiness involves external circumstances.

The right person has to be around you, the right people have to be doing the right things, you must be feeling the right range of emotions, the right results are happening. Whatever the case may be, the way most people define happiness involves some sort of process where things from the outside are influencing the things you're feeling on the inside. This is a serious problem.

The reason should be obvious. We can't control what's going on in the outside world. We can't control how people act, we can't control what they say, we can't control the outcomes of our actions despite our best efforts.

We can increase the likelihood that we would be successful. We could increase the chances that we will get the results that we are looking for, but it's not a slam dunk. There are no guarantees.

So what do you do? Are you going to fall down and crumple into a ball and cry because things aren't working out the way you'd want them to?

I know this sounds comedic, but this exactly how a lot of people respond. They basically throw a tantrum. They say, "It's unfair. Everybody else sucks."

You're more than welcome to feel that way, but let me tell you, it's not going to change anything. This is why pursuing happiness, in and of itself, often leads to a dead end. You have to redefine it.

I'm not saying that you should let go of the concept altogether. Nobody's arguing for that. Instead, you need to start changing your attitude about happiness.

Unfortunately, far too many of us think that happiness is some sort of commodity or product. If I buy something, I will be happy. If I buy that car that shows up on that TV ad late at night, I will be happy. If I meet this special person, I would be happy.

Do you see the logical structure of the past three statements that I just said? If something happens or if a product is consumed, then you are happy.

This is a serious problem because it doesn't work that way. Maybe you don't have the money, maybe you hang around with the wrong people, or maybe your situation is just set up differently.

Whatever the case may be, if you keep repeating this logic that if x happens, then happiness will flow, you're going to be stuck. And the worst part is that you're doing it to yourself.

Happiness is Not a Destination Either

I remember when I was in high school and everybody was preoccupied with going to the high school dance, getting drunk afterwards, partying, and smoking weed.

Instead, I said to myself, "I need to study hard. I need to get accepted into the right colleges. I need to sign up to the right programs, and I will be happy." Sure enough, I got into a good university after high school.

At that point, everybody was excited about the homecoming football games. People were throwing block parties. Everybody was having a great time, but there I was, locked in the library because I had this idea that once I get that great corporate job after college, I will be happy.

The price I have to pay, however, is that I have to get really good grades. I have to graduate in the top 20% of my class. So I decided to pay that price and guess what happened? I graduated with honors, and I got my first corporate job at a big company.

Was I happy? Well, pay attention to the pattern. I wasn't. By that time, I had my eyes fixed on graduate school.

The reason for this sad story is a faulty mindset. I defined happiness as some sort of destination that I had to work towards. So once I reached that destination, I would be happy.

Well, here's the problem. When I went through that process, I ended up kicking the can further down the road.

I was kind of like a horse with a stick tied around my head and at the end of the stick, a foot or two from my nose, is a carrot. No matter how hard I run after that carrot, I will never get close to eating it. It's just not going to happen.

As funny as that image may be, it leads to tragedy. Seriously.

What is the tragedy? Well, in high school, I didn't have many happy memories because I was always in the library. My friends were having a good time, they were enjoying their lives, they were exploring life.

Sure, they made bad decisions from time to time, but that's the way it works. You become stronger because you see how life works.

Often times, your parents can tell you that it's a rough world out there, but until and unless you see and feel it for yourself because of your bad decision, you're never going to learn.

I sealed myself off from that. It was even worse in college because everybody else was having a great time. People were going on long road trips, finding themselves, questioning the world, questioning what they thought about the world, questioning their parents, questioning religion, and all that, and then they came out more balanced people.

And guess what? Those people are now doctors, judges, lawyers, politicians, business owners, you name it.

My point here is that happiness is not some sort of destination because the more you push towards it, the more distant it becomes.

Choose Positivity Instead

Instead of looking at happiness as some sort of product or some sort of destination, look at it in alternative terms. Focus less on being happy. Instead, focus more on being positive.

When you're positive, it doesn't necessarily mean that you have the brightest smile on your face. It doesn't necessarily mean that you're walking on cloud nine and hugging and kissing and embracing everybody that you meet.

It doesn't have to be that because, hey, let's face it, the world is full of hostile, mean and rough people. I'm just telling you the truth. No amount of imagination is going to make this unpleasant truth go away.

That's just the way life is. Life is rough, it's unfair, and it can get downright mean and chaotic. But when you choose positivity, you always look at the victory in every situation.

This gives you a sense of perspective. You don't look for that elusive unicorn of happiness. And once you find out that it's not in the picture, you get depressed or you get cynical and want to burn the whole thing down.

Instead, when you adopt a positive mindset, you gain perspective. Because even in the bleakest of situations, you can still have control and power.

I know that sounds crazy, I know that cuts against the grain of everything that you have been told up to this point, but it's absolutely true. You only need to look at the works of famous psychologist Victor Frankel.

He wrote a book called "Man's Search for Meaning" and he told a very horrendous story of being a prisoner in a Nazi concentration camp. But even in that bleak, seemingly hopeless environment, he saw acts of kindness. He saw glimmers of joy.

Why? People chose to find meaning where they are. They chose to interpret their situation in the best way possible without lying to themselves.

This is the power of positivity. Because in any given situation, it's not 100% black, nor 100% white. It's not 100% pain or 100% joy.

Life being the way it is, there's always elements of gray. It's always a combination.

This means that there is something to be positive about.

The fact that you can choose to respond in a positive way or in a controlled way instead of just running around like a chicken with your head cut off because everything has fallen apart and there's really no hope, is a source of optimism.

In other words, the fact that you still have the ability to respond in a neutral, if not positive way, is an affirmation of your personal power over your reality. This is good news. This is what positivity teaches.

In a study done by UC Berkeley professor Iris Mauss, actively searching for happiness is usually a dead end. In the study, the researchers told participants to feel happier while they're watching a nice film clip. They then measured the emotional state of the people after watching that clip. They actually felt worse.

In other words, the more you pursue happiness, either as some sort of commodity or some sort of destination, the worse off you feel.

In a study conducted by Lana Catalino, a postdoctoral researcher at the psychiatry department in the University of California at San Francisco School of Medicine, focusing on positivity yielded better results because when you do this, you let go of wanting to feel happy all the time.

Instead, you just focus on finding what's best or what's hopeful in any situation. You unburden yourself of a tremendous amount of pressure. Apparently, the more you let go, the better you perform when doing a task or when brainstorming.

Many psychologists call this mental state a "state of flow." This is a high level of personal competence. You're just able to just do a lot of tasks that normally would weigh you down or would normally be difficult, very easily. This is marked by a state where you lose self awareness.

This is the complete opposite of trying to be happy. Because when you're looking for that happiness moment, you focus on yourself. You're always thinking to yourself, "Am I happy now? Am I getting the happiness that

I'm looking for? Am I in a state of happiness?"

This is different from "flow" because when you're in "flow," you're just focused outside of you. You're focused on helping another person. You're focused on solving somebody else's problem. You're focused on the world of ideas, which doesn't revolve around your ego. It leads to an explosion of a sense of possibility.

Positivity also means reflecting on activities that give you contentment or joy. You focus on the activity, you don't focus on getting happiness from that. And according to Catalino's research, this led to better results. This led to less stress.

Chapter 7: Redefine Happiness

Please understand that, as I mentioned in the previous chapter, happiness is not something that you possess. It's not some sort of state that comes from the outside and overtakes you. It is definitely not some sort of destination.

Regardless of which conventional definition you use, having wealth or material things doesn't define happiness.

By freeing yourself from this tendency to view happiness as some sort of commodity and redefine it as an experience, you are more likely to achieve an emotional state that is more empowering. I wouldn't call it happiness because it just has too much baggage, but you would definitely achieve a better state of mind.

The problem with defining happiness as some sort of commodity is that sooner or later, the commodity runs out.

It's kind of like eating rice, donuts, mashed potatoes, bread, or anything that has a lot of carbs. You get this nice sugar rush. Your glycemic index spikes up, and then it crashes down. So you're hungry again. This repeats over and over again.

It's also similar to eating a candy bar. It's loaded with sugar and you get this nice sugar high. You get the picture.

You end up chasing your tail. It's a dead end. It has no point.

Start redefining happiness as an experience.

In the Purdue study I mentioned in an earlier chapter, experiences last longer than goods when it comes to personal states of happiness. It's very easy to see why.

You can buy an experience, true enough. After all, plane tickets cost money. Hotel rooms cost money. Access to a beach often costs money. But everything else is up to you.

When you define happiness as involving experiences, your ability to make sense of the world and read your own personal meaning into the things happening around you and to you is triggered.

According to that Purdue study, people tend to be happier if they focus on experiences. What this tells us is that when people engage in some sort of activity that somehow triggers their built-in ability to remember, prioritize and interpret or analyze things that happened to them, they tend to be happier.

It is not really the experience itself that triggers the happiness. Instead, it's your reading of what happened.

Believe it or not, a lot of people have happy memories of experiences that did not involve high ticket items or expensive vacations. They don't have to be doing anything particularly special.

A friend of mine once told me that some of the happiest memories of her life which still brings a smile to her face to this very day was when she would sleep in her bed right next to a washer and dryer machine.

During that time of her life, her parents were just getting started. They couldn't afford a big place. They couldn't even afford a formal house.

They lived in a building that had washers and dryers and the room that they rented had a few of these machines. They were paying really low rent.

Even though they moved on to a much bigger house and enjoyed all the finer things in life, she fondly remembers that time she lived in that room.

She would tell me, with a nostalgic glint in her eyes, the sound the dryer would make. She said that when she was a kid, it bothered her at first, but after a while, it became part of her world.

When she was going through any kind of challenge when she was older, maybe it was in college or graduate school, she'd always think back to how that dryer sounded and a flood of comforting memories would come over her. She drew on that memory as a source of strength, support and hope.

My point is that you can develop memories from just about anything. It's how you read these memories, and the lessons you get out of them, that give you power.

At the end of the day, it's not really the memory itself. It's how you choose to read them. It all boils down to the interpretation that you have selected for them.

My friend Amy could have easily interpreted her childhood spent in that storehouse as the worst in her life. It can be a period of humiliation, degradation, oppression, you name it. It could be some sort of memory she would continuously try to run away from because it was so bleak, hopeless and degrading.

Instead, she fondly mimics the woomp-woomp-woomp sound as she was telling me that story. Obviously, there is a special part in her heart for that experience.

And this is not hard wired because two people living the same facts would walk away with two totally different interpretations. That happy memory is Amy's interpretation. Her sister Janet could have a completely different interpretation. I hope you get my point.

When you redefine happiness, you make it work for you. You make it part of your agenda. It becomes a tool. It becomes an extension of your built-in ability to define your reality. I'll go into this in further detail in Chapter 8.

But please understand that your life is not a foregone conclusion. You're not some sort of passive observer or moviegoer of your life where you just sit back and watch the movie of your life play out in front of your eyes.

You can't lift a finger to change what happens on the screen because that would be fruitless. You basically just sit back and take whatever the movie dishes out at you.

You're powerless. You have no control. You're mute. You have no say in the matter. You're voiceless.

Well, that's not the truth. The truth is, we are constantly making and remaking reality.

Just by being alive, you are processing the thousands upon thousands of stimuli hitting your senses every second and picking out what's important and what's not. You choose what you want to remember and discard everything else.

What do you do with the things that you choose to hang on to? That's right, you fit that into this narrative or grand script you have of your existence called your identity. That's how it works. That's how everything fits together.

And at the center of that process is you. You are in control.

I know that's news to a lot of people because it seems that their lives are just spiraling out of control and they are at the mercy of people and circumstances that are beyond their control. But pay attention to this fact: you can always choose how you respond. Nobody can take that away from you.

As I have mentioned earlier, the psychiatrist Victor Frankel was in a Nazi concentration camp and he tapped into his ability to find meaning even in the bleakest of situations.

In other words, he took ownership over his natural ability to define his reality or read meaning into his reality.

This will always stay with you. It will always be there. But the only question is, are you going to claim it? Are you going to take ownership of it?

It's like a gift. It has nice wrapping paper, it has a nice bow, but that gift will only work if you take off the wrapper and unpack it and use it.

In a total of eight studies, Cornell University research psychologists Thomas Gilovich and Travis Carter noticed that people who spent money on experiences, like trips and vacations, reported being happier for a longer period of time than people who bought stuff.

It turns out that when consumers buy stuff, they get a nice initial rush. But when they quickly adapt to the stuff that they bought, their sense of fulfillment drops like a rock. This happens like clockwork.

The main reason for this is because they compare the stuff that they bought with what they already have or they second guess themselves regarding their decision. They're thinking to themselves, "Why did I buy this instead of something else? How does this purchase compare to somebody else's?"

The end result is the same. People are not satisfied.

The researchers call this the adaptation level theory. Basically, we quickly adapt and get used to our product choices and instead of feeling really good that you bought something that you thought you could not afford before, you strip yourself of all the fulfillment that that item could have given you because you compared it to something else or to other people.

From a personal perspective, this is especially true when it comes to houses and cars. There is such a thing as keeping up with the Joneses.

When a neighbor rolls in with a brand new Mercedes, what do you think happens? That's right, there's a predictable tidal wave where Mercedes Benzes or BMWs start popping up in the neighborhood's garages. Everybody achieves the same level, and then any sense of satisfaction is wiped clean, and then the process repeats itself again.

When you purchase life experiences, on the other hand, like training courses or vacation trips, there is less comparison because your trip is yours. The meaning that you give to your trip, what it triggers, how you interpret your trip, that's all yours.

So you know deep down inside that you really cannot compare how you felt about that trip to somebody else who made the same trip. Two people could go to Paris, France but walk away with totally different interpretations.

You know that everybody's entitled to their interpretation when they experience something, so you're less likely to suffer from adaptation level theory.

Chapter 8: Choose to Edit Your Life

Movies need editing to unleash their power. Have you ever watched a movie being made? It's kind of puzzling.

The director would take some shots of parts of a scene. Different staff members would shoot the actors at different times and at different places. It's really hard to put it all together because it seems like there are so many things happening at the same time.

It's easy to get confused. It's easy to think that, "No way is this a movie because it seems that it's so disjointed, disconnected and chaotic."

Sure enough, when the movie trailer comes out, you get all excited because the movie trailer captures certain parts of the film that excite you. So you pay money to see the movie and you treat yourself to a well-made movie. It truly delivers whatever the trailer promises.

This is how most movies work. Of course, there are exceptions to this. I don't need to remind you that there are really bad movies out there. But by and large, this is how movies work.

Often times, the final work that you see on the screen looks extremely different and feels extremely different from the movie that you saw being filmed. What's the secret? Editing.

Make no mistake, movies, novels, essays, or most other creative artworks need editing to be effective. There are all sorts of bits and pieces that are flying all over the place. This is especially true when it comes to writing.

When you're writing, you have so many ideas flying at the speed of light through your mind. Your neurons can barely process them.

In fact, a lot of them just hit you in the form of feelings. Your mind isn't able to whip them into some sort of coherent form. They just hit you from all over the place.

You have to make some sort of judgment call. You have to prioritize things. You have to make sense of all this chaos.

This is why editing is so powerful. You just basically dump everything that you want to say on a blank piece of paper, and then you go line by line cutting stuff out, moving stuff up, moving stuff down, setting stuff apart.

Throughout this whole process, you try to keep your focus on the big picture. What are you trying to say? What is the thesis? What is the argument?

Or if you're writing fiction, what is the arc of the story? How do I tie what's going on in this scene to my character sketch? What kind of truths am I trying to share?

Editing is crucial to all of this because it helps you get rid of all the errors, the dead ends, the half-baked ideas, or the flashy impulses that lead nowhere.

Sound familiar? Well, it should be because your life is not an exception. You have to cut out the extras to focus on the real stuff.

And, believe it or not, you have the power to edit your life. How do you do this? Well, the first step is to let go of guilt.

Let's face it, we're not perfect. There is no such thing as a perfect person. That animal never existed. We were imperfect in the past, we're imperfect now, and we'll continue to be imperfect for the foreseeable future.

Understand this fact and move on. You have to let go of guilt and your tendency to hang on to past mistakes that hold you down and keep you back from the kind of life you could otherwise be enjoying.

How do you do this? Well, first of all, you have to forgive yourself for wasting all that time, effort and mental energy relitigating past harms and bad moves on your part or other people's part.

Either we're the ones being harmed or we're the ones doing the harming. Whatever the case may be, if you keep tossing around these mental images, you are engaged in guilt. You keep coming back over and over to the stuff that happened in the past.

What's wrong with this picture? It should be obvious.

I don't know of anybody who has access to some sort of time machine. Life is not the "Back to the Future" movie series. You're not Marty McFly. You don't have access to this amazing Delorean with gull wings that can help you go back to the past.

Life doesn't work that way. Whatever happened already happened.

It doesn't matter how many times you keep showing that mental movie to yourself, it's not going to change. It already happened. It already had an impact. What you can change is how you interpret what happened in the past.

The facts took place, whether you like it or not and whether you accept them or not. What's important is you take ownership of your power to understand and interpret those facts.

Because, unfortunately, a lot of people rob themselves of positivity and a sense of possibility because they keep interpreting things that happened in the past in the worst way possible. They hold themselves back. They keep themselves prisoner to their past mistakes or to the past harms done to them by other people.

The Process of Letting Go

To let go of the past so you can edit your life more efficiently and more effectively, you need to ask for forgiveness. Forgive yourself and ask for forgiveness from people that you've harmed.

Let Go of Guilt

The next step is to let go of guilt. Guilt can only go away if you go through forgiveness.

Either you forgive yourself or you forgive others, or others forgive you, or a combination of these. Whatever the case may be, there has to be some objective indication of forgiveness.

Because when you forgive, you operate on many different levels. You mentally forgive, you emotionally forgive, and you verbally forgive.

So there's a physical aspect to this. This is not just something that's flashing in and out in your mind. This is real.

You have to forgive yourself. You have to unclench and let go.

Let It Sink In

Here's the heavy part. It's one thing to intellectually realize certain things in life, it's another to actually live it out. You probably don't need me to remind you of this.

There are many things that we can all mentally agree on. There are so many things that we know we should do, so we kind of clarify things intellectually. But we tend to compartmentalize things, so there seems to be a big divide between what we think about and what we really feel.

Similarly, there is a distinction between what we verbally say we can accept and what we accept to live with.

You have to get rid of that wall. You have to let it sink in. This has to be real.

Because it's not real when you're just repeating this mantra to yourself that past sex abuse, past humiliation by your boss, or past crimes you committed against others are dead and buried. You can do that until you're blue in the face, but it's not going to do you much good until and unless it changes how you feel about them.

So your emotional state has to change. If you do this, it leads to the things that you routinely talk about. That has to change as well.

If you stick to this forgiveness pattern enough, it also changes how you behave. And that's when things get real.

Why? Well, the world doesn't really care about what you feel. Everybody's got feelings. The world only sits up and pays attention to what you do.

We live in a results-based world. Everybody can talk a good game, but guess what? The world pays attention to people who could actually do it.

There is quite a bit of science about forgiveness. One particular study stands out. This was conducted by psychology researchers at Baylor University.

They set up an experiment to test the impact of forgiveness. They tried to analyze where the forgiveness process starts. Sure enough, it doesn't start with forgiving others first. Instead, it starts with forgiving ourselves.

"Forgiving ourselves for hurting another is easier if we make amends."

According to this research from Baylor University, we have to make amends. We have to seek forgiveness because this makes it easier to forgive ourselves.

But from a practical perspective, you have to start with forgiving yourself first so as to open the door to asking for forgiveness. Because without that, it's going to be very hard.

It really will be because it's very easy to paint yourself as some sort of victim. It's very easy to find all sorts of excuses and justifications.

So we have to make some sort of decision at first that we seek forgiveness and we seek it first from ourselves, at least in terms of a commitment, and then we do the hard part, which is asking for forgiveness from others.

Once you do this, this makes the first part even more powerful. You can then revisit your forgiveness of yourself and deepen it because you get a moral okay when you do this. It puts everything in perspective.

In another study published through INSEAD, people who have a tough time forgiving can develop a victim mindset. This is very, very toxic and can cause all sorts of problems.

Believe it or not, people who turn out to be horrific victimizers often view themselves as victims themselves.

This INSEAD research released in 2012 shows that the victim mindset syndrome leads people to a self defeating cycle because when people feel that bad things constantly happen to them, the less in control they feel. This leads to even worse things happening because they have basically let go of that control.

To make matters worse, it also gives them some sort of excuse to victimize other people because they keep going back to the idea that they themselves are victims.

It's not a surprise, according to the study, that people who view themselves as victims end up hurting people who are actually trying to help them. This should be familiar to people who are stuck in codependent relationships.

Chapter 9: Clean Space is Vital

Having clean space around you is important. But to get that clean space, you have to make a decision.

Geographic space is a choice. You can always choose to clean up or not.

And it doesn't really matter how much initial space you begin with. You may live in a cramped apartment, but you keep it nice and spacious.

Objectively speaking, there's not enough square meters or square feet in your living quarters, but that's okay. If you proactively keep your space clean, it would feel like you have more space.

Similarly, you can have a fairly large space by any objective measure, but if you let clutter pile up quickly because you feel you're too busy, you feel trapped. Soon enough, you feel stuck that there's not enough space.

The same phenomena also plays out when it comes to cleanliness. When you keep stuff dirty or you let stuff get dirty or let grime and dust pile up because you feel that you just don't have the time, you become more and more stressed.

Whether you like it or not, cleanliness leads to higher levels of mental comfort and less stress. Survey studies bear this out.

In a study conducted by the National Sleep Foundation, people who have made it a habit to routinely get their beds in order after they wake up in the morning are 19% more likely to report that they had a good night's sleep.

When looking at the cleanliness of the sheets, the National Sleep Foundation survey participants said that they had a better quality sleep when their sheets are nice and clean. They feel that the sheets are fresh. They associated this with a feeling of comfort.

In a study out of the United Kingdom, people who have very cluttered and messy desks showed a 77% fall in productivity.

Their motivation was also negatively affected. In fact, in the same study involving subjective mental states that are self reported, when people have messy surroundings, their happiness drops by 40%.

Final Word

Jordan Peterson is a very famous Canadian psychologist and professor at the University of Toronto. He recently released a book titled "12 Rules for Life." One of the chapters is titled "Clean Your Room."

On the surface, this might seem very banal or almost ridiculously routine. But Professor Peterson's point is very powerful.

If you want to assert more control over your life, stop trying to change the world. Stop trying to get other people to think differently. Stop trying to make big waves to reach the most remote centers of power. Stop making grand statements.

Instead, clean your room. Focus on what's in front of you.

He said that the simple act is actually harder than people realize. Because it's precisely the everyday, the routine, the banal, that reflects our mindset. It reflects our priorities. It reflects our values.

And by actively changing your surroundings, you start changing internally. You become more proactive. You take the initiative more. Most importantly, you tap into your personal power to make changes in your life.

People who keep saying "What happened" or "It's not fair" have lost sight of the fact that they have this power to make changes in their life. They stay so focused on the perceived enemies or bad people making bad things happen in their lives that they lost sight of the fact that they themselves can start chain reactions using everyday decisions.

Professor Peterson also warned that when you make a change, people will oppose you. I know, it sounds so basic. You're repainting your room, you're cleaning everything out, why would people oppose you?

Well, they would oppose you because you are reasserting your power over your life. This is a reminder to them that they have that same power. They can get their act together as well, but they don't want to. They don't want to change.

Accordingly, they see what you're doing with your life as a threat, so they will put up all sorts of objections, justifications, reasons, and stumbling blocks because they know that the moment you achieve success with something as basic as cleaning up your room, the ball goes to their court. Because if you can do it, they can do it too.

But they don't want to. They don't want to let go. They want to hang on. They want to believe in the lies and misconceptions and myths they keep telling themselves over and over, so you become a threat.

Don't think for a second that this is easy stuff. It isn't. Because clean space, while being vital, is also a product of internal, and sometimes external, struggle. Be prepared for that.

Chapter 10: Best Practices

What follows are some best practices you need to wrap your mind around.

You have to understand that the principles outlined above need to be carried out. Otherwise, they're just ideas bouncing around in your head.

They're not going to do anybody a bit of good until and unless you carry them out. You have to implement them.

Here are some best practices that would enable you to live out the 6 principles of minimalism sooner rather than later.

Commitment

Minimalism requires commitment. You can't just declutter this second, and then the next minute you're hoarding back irrelevant things. Commitment really means taking the power of decision back.

If you're reading this book, at some level or another, you feel that you're not in control of your life. At some level or another, you feel that things just spiral out of control and there's really nothing you can say or do about it.

Well, when you choose to commit by deciding right here, right now that things are going to change, you start taking power over your life.

One of the most important powers you will always have, and that nobody can take away from you, is the power to decide. Here's an extreme example.

Let's say you are in your house and there is a massive earthquake. Everything is destroyed around you. There are fires breaking out, people are losing their lives, it's a mess. Do you think that you have power at that moment?

Surprisingly, the answer is "yes." You have the power to decide your response.

There are two ways to play this. You can choose, like most people, to run around like a chicken with its head cut off. You basically say, "Ahh, it's the end of the world! Everything's messed up!"

What do you think will happen? A whole lot of nothing because everybody else is doing that. It's chaos.

The other way you can play this is to shut up and calmly assess the situation. You start going through a checklist in your mind. Where do I find water? What safe place can I gather everybody? What kind of things need to be done right now to get help, protect ourselves, and get resources?

Believe it or not, when you think in this calm, orderly manner, things get done. Why? Those people running around like chickens that got decapitated, they're actually looking for guidance. They're looking for a point of stability.

When they see somebody ordering people and organizing everybody, they get that stability. They calm down. They become part of the solution instead of prolonging the problem.

All this goes back to decision. Decide that you're going to take control of your life right now.

Remember that you always have the power to decide. You always have a choice on how you respond to the stimuli of the outside world.

Purpose

Declutter everything that does not add meaning. Always understand that everything has to fit a grand picture for your life. Everything that you put in that picture must have meaning. This should be the central organizing principle of your life.

You have to always ask yourself, "Will buying this stuff add to my personal meaning? Is this a reflection of the meaning that I've chosen for myself?"

I wish I could tell you that there is some sort of bright line, black and white answer here, but I don't know you personally. You have to decide. You have to define what your personal purpose is.

What is your life's meaning? Where is this all leading to for you? What kind of destiny do you see for yourself?

Come to an Agreement

If you are in a relationship and you want to take action on the principles outlined in this book, please understand that you are not living just for yourself. If you're in a relationship, there is a third party in that arrangement.

That's right. There is a third party. And I'm not talking about your partner being unfaithful with a third party. I'm talking about the relationship itself.

When you commit to that person, whether you're married or not, there is a third party born. That third party is the relationship. This means that you're going to have to sacrifice part of what makes you happy and a tremendous amount of expediency for the interest of that third party.

In other words, both partners give up certain things so that the relationship can grow. That's how you know you are in a responsible, adult, mature relationship because there is mutual sacrifice.

This means that you are able to continue loving your partner even though they dropped the ball, even though they don't treat you well all the time, or even if they say very negative things or they've done bad things.

Why? Because your loyalty is not necessarily to that person, but to the relationship.

And if this is mutual, then you have yourself a recipe for a successful relationship. But if this exchange is not there and you're not both at the same level of maturity, then there's going to be an issue.

And one way you grow that maturity is when you discuss with your partner and make sure that that person buys into what you're trying to achieve with this book.

Cultivate Inner Space

In addition to letting go of stuff physically, let go of your inner clutter. Cultivate tremendous space in your life.

Because when you feel that you have a lot of space in your heart and a lot of space in your personal psychology, you're able to give more. You're able to be more patient with others. It's as if you have a lot more rope to work with.

Nobody can give that to you. You have to give it to yourself. The best way to do this, of course, is to make space internally.

Conclusion

Minimalism is quickly becoming popular in the United States and Western Europe. It is making particularly great inroads among millennials.

Whatever your reasons may be for adopting minimalism, please understand that it is a journey. It is not some sort of product that you buy that leads to instant transformation.

Let go of that toxic idea because you will only be disappointed in the end. Instead, look at it as a fun journey that you're going on. And just like any other journey, there will be frustrations along the way.

If you've ever gone on a road trip, there are times when you realize that you did not buy what you needed to buy at the convenience store at your previous stop. It would probably be another hundred miles before you get to the next store.

Similarly, you may be in a journey with people that may rub you the wrong way. There might be disagreements.

Whatever the case may be, please understand that on this journey, the process is the purpose. It's not the destination. It's the fact that you have made yourself available to change, that is the victory. That is what you're aiming for.

You're opening up. You're not looking to become a totally better person or you're trying to measure how much of a changed person you would be. Those are great and everything, but focus on what's important. Focus on the fact that the process changes you as you yourself take action on the process.

I wish you nothing but an amazing journey.

Copyright © 2018 by Nick Anderson

All rights reserved. No part of this book may be reproduced in any form without permission in writing from the author.

No part of this publication may be reproduced or transmitted in any form or by any means, mechanical or electronic, including photocopying or recording, or by any information storage and retrieval system, or transmitted by email or by any other means whatsoever without permission in writing from the author.

DISCLAIMER

While all attempts have been made to verify the information provided in this publication, the author does not assume any responsibility for errors, omissions, or contrary interpretations of the subject matter herein.

The views expressed are those of the author alone and should not be taken as expert instruction or commands. The reader is responsible for his or her own actions.

The author makes no representations or warranties with respect to the accuracy or completeness of the contents of this work and specifically disclaims all warranties, including without limitation warranties of fitness for a particular purpose. No warranty may be created or extended by sales or promotional materials. The advice and recipes contained herein may not be suitable for everyone. This work is sold with the understanding that the author is not engaged in rendering medical, legal or other professional advice or services. If professional assistance is required, the services of a competent professional person should be sought. The author shall not be liable for damages arising here from. The fact that an individual, organization of website is referred to in this work as a citation and/or potential source of further information does not mean that the author endorses the information the individual, organization to website may provide or recommendations they/it may make. Further, readers should be aware that Internet websites listed in this work might have changed or disappeared between when this work was written and when it is read.

Adherence to all applicable laws and regulations, including international, federal, state, and local governing professional licensing, business practices, advertising, and all other aspects of doing business in any jurisdiction in the world is the sole responsibility of the purchaser or reader.

Made in the USA
Columbia, SC
14 October 2018